poems and paintings by

Douglas Florian

harcourt, inc.

SAN DIEGO • NEW YORK • LONDON

lizards, frogs, and polliwogs

www.harcourt.com

Library of Congress Cataloging-in-Publication Data
Florian, Douglas.
Lizards, frogs, and polliwogs: poems and paintings/
by Douglas Florian.—1st ed.
p.   cm.
Summary: A collection of humorous poems about such reptiles and
amphibians as the glass frog, the gecko, and the rattlesnake.
1. Reptiles—Juvenile poetry.   2. Amphibians—Juvenile poetry.
3. Children's Poetry, American.   [1. Reptiles—Poetry.
2. Amphibians—Poetry.   3. American poetry.   4. Humorous poetry.]
I. Title.
PS3556.L589L59   2001
811'.54—dc21   99-50830
ISBN 0-15-202591-X

First edition

A C E G H F D B

PRINTED IN HONG KONG

Contents

The Skink

Along the ground I'm found—I slink.
Through grass I pass—I am a skink.
Bite my tail and it releases.
I don't fight back—
I *fall to pieces.*

7

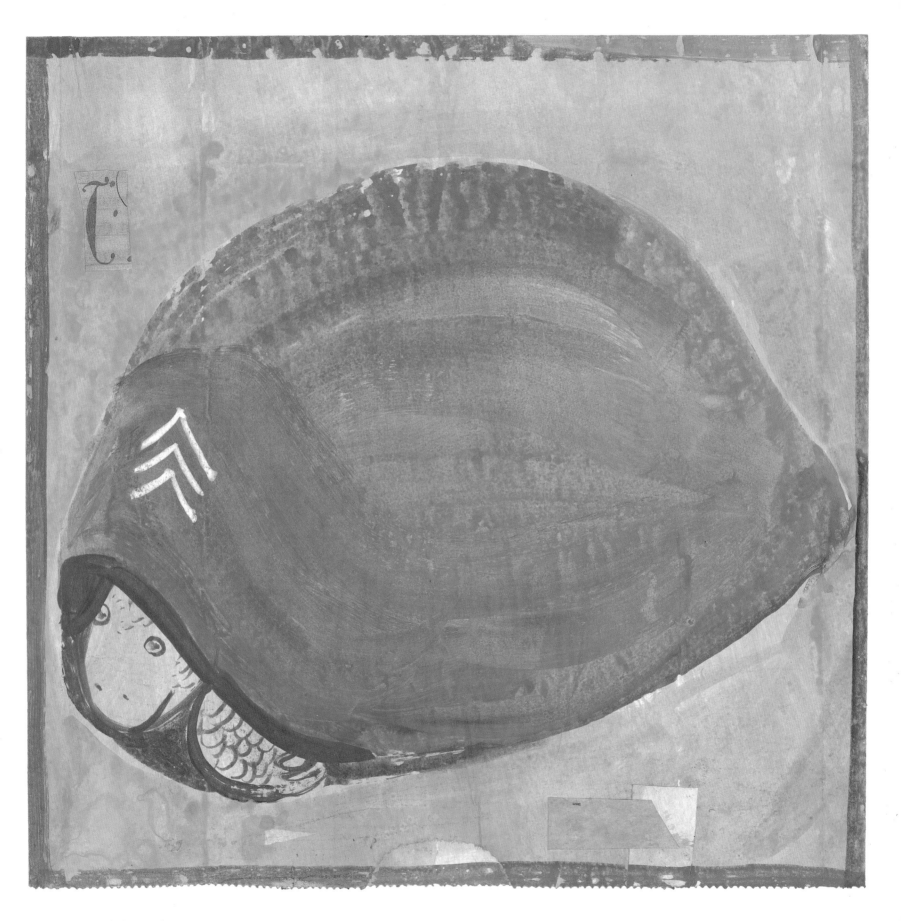

The Tortoise

I wear a helmet
On my back.
It's hard
And guards
Me from attack.
And if I wheeze,
      Or sneeze,
          Or cough,
The shell I dwell in
Won't fall off.
It's glued without
A screw or mortise.
I'm born with it,
For I'm a tortoise.

Across the ceiling it may roam,

Like glue it sticks and rarely falls.

But don't you try this in your home.

The gecko's trick is climbing walls.

The Gecko

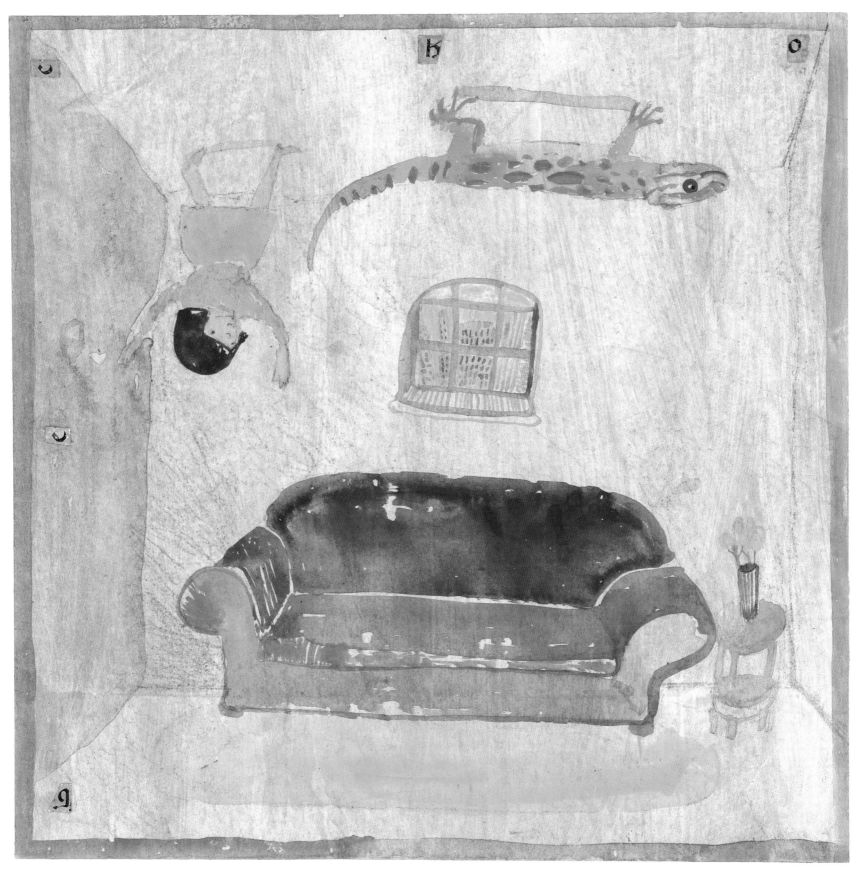

11

The Crocodile and the Alligator

The crocodile's smile is wide
Enough to stuff a pig inside.
But did you know that alligators
Sometimes swallow second graders?

The Iguana

I wouldn't wanna
Be an iguana—
Iguanas are covered with scales.

I wouldn't wanna
Be an iguana—
Iguanas can have spiny tails.

I wouldn't wanna
Be an iguana—
Iguanas are sometimes green.

I wouldn't wanna
Be an iguana—
Except for Halloween.

15

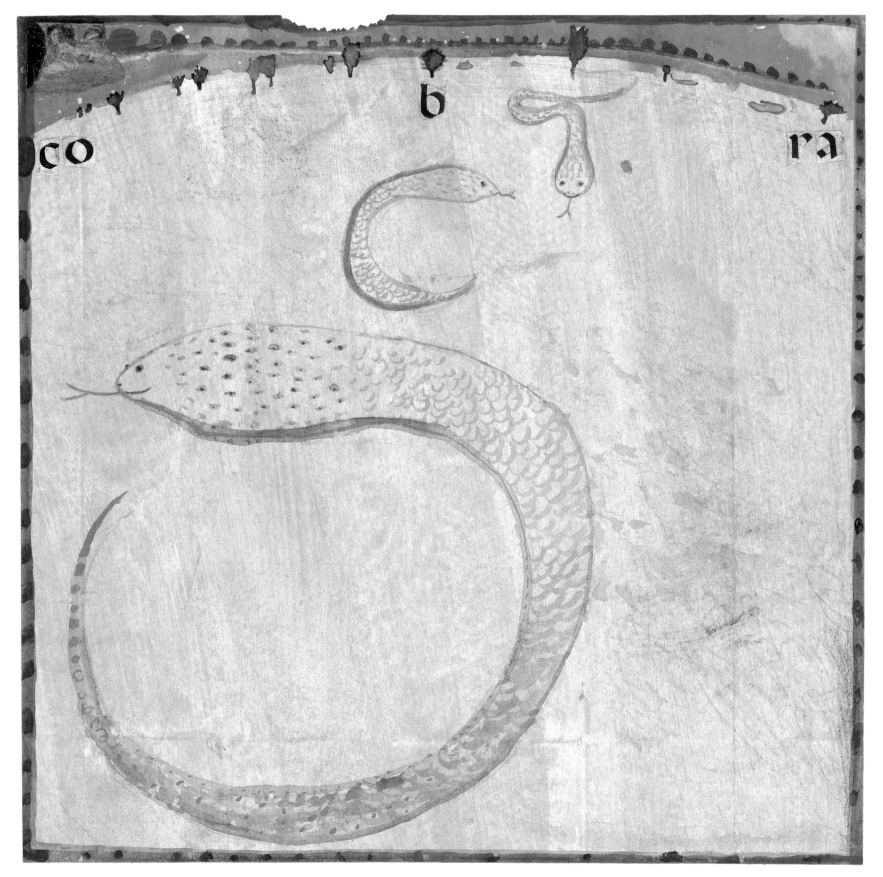

The Cobra

It's wise to stay clear
      Of the dangerous cobra
All months of the year,
      Including Octobra.

The Komodo Dragon

I am komodo.
I'm gruesome and gray—
The most massive lizard
That's living today.
Birds and boars
For me are a meal,
Plus all those who don't think
That dragons are real.

The Gila Monster

They call me monster just because
I have short legs and clumsy claws,
And poison in my jaws,
And look
Like someone's composition book.

The Box Turtle

This bony dome's
My mobile home,
A shell
So swell
In which to roam.
And when I'm scared
By bear or fox,
Inside I hide
Safe in my box.
I close it shut
And go to bed,
Secure from beasts
That *box* my head.

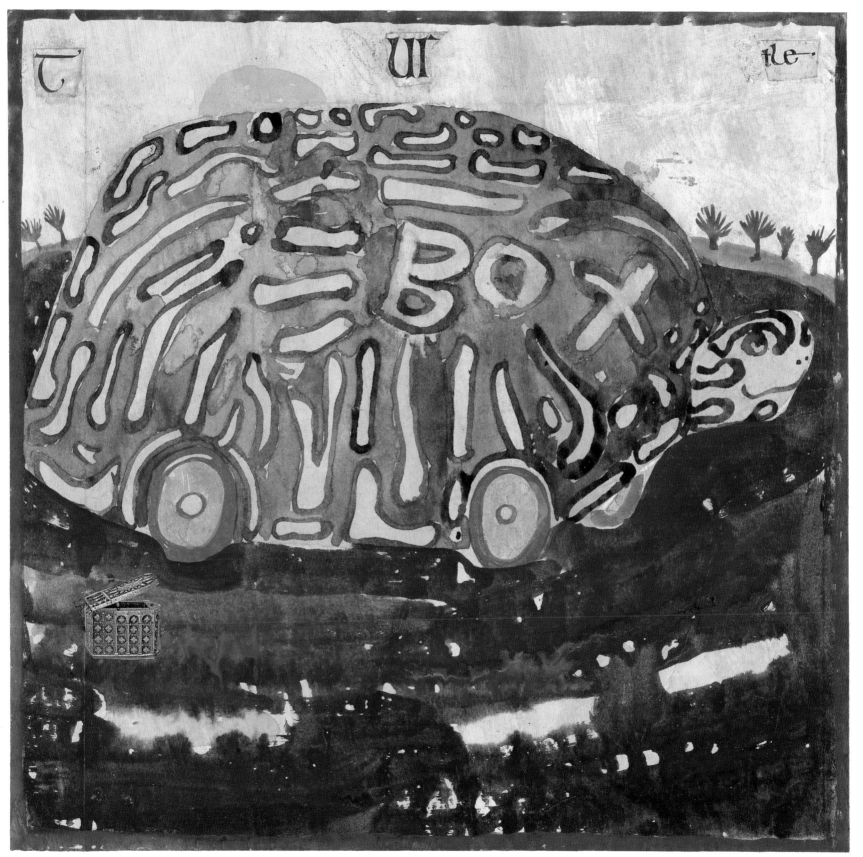

23

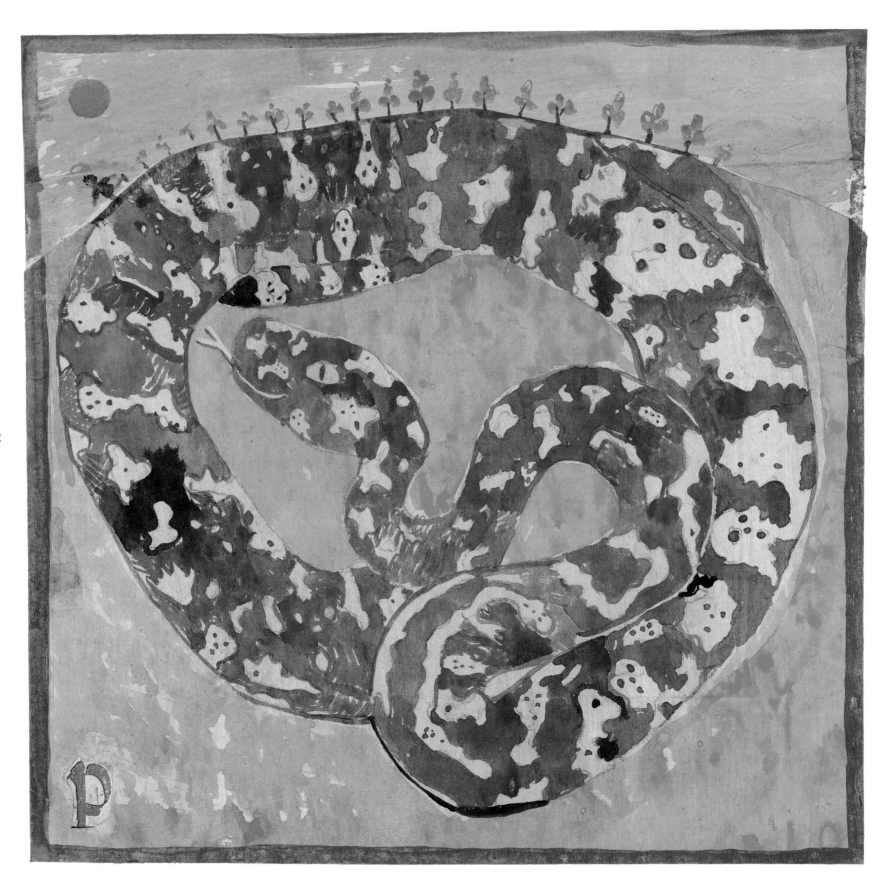

The Python

With thirty feet to squeeze your prey, Python, you take my breath away!

The Chameleon

Chameleon, comedian,
We never know which skin you're in.
Sometimes you're yellow,
Then you're green,
Turquoise blue, or tangerine.
Chameleon, you're hard to find.
Comedian, make up your mind!

27

28

The Diamondback
Rattlesnake

Fork in front,
Rattle behind.
The lump in the middle?
Don't pay any mind.

Scales up high,
Scales down low.
The lump in the middle?
You don't want to know.

Diamonds above,
Diamonds below.
The lump in the middle?
A rabbit too slow.

The Polliwogs

We polliwoggle.
We polliwiggle.
We shake in lakes,
Make wakes,
And wriggle.
We quiver,
We shiver,
We jiggle,
We jog.
We're yearning
To turn ourselves
Into a frog.

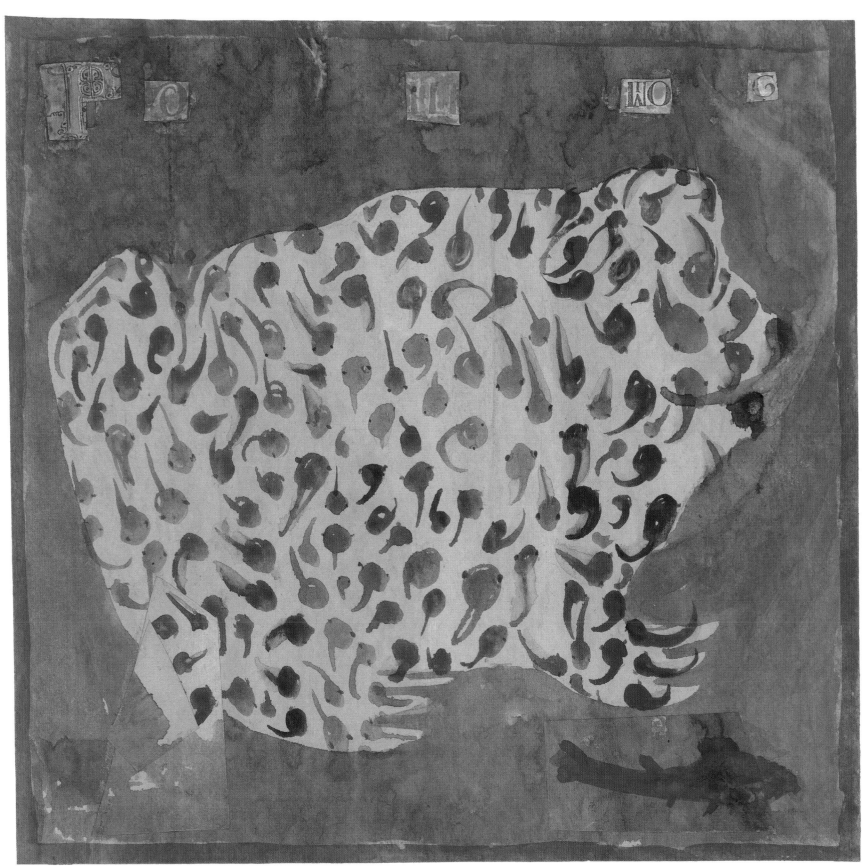

32

The Midwife Toad

On Dad's back the eggs are toted.
To his kids he's *toadally* devoted.

The Glass Frog

Upon a tree
It's hard to see
Which part is leaf
And which is me
Which part is me
And which is leaf
I've lost myself again—
Good grief!

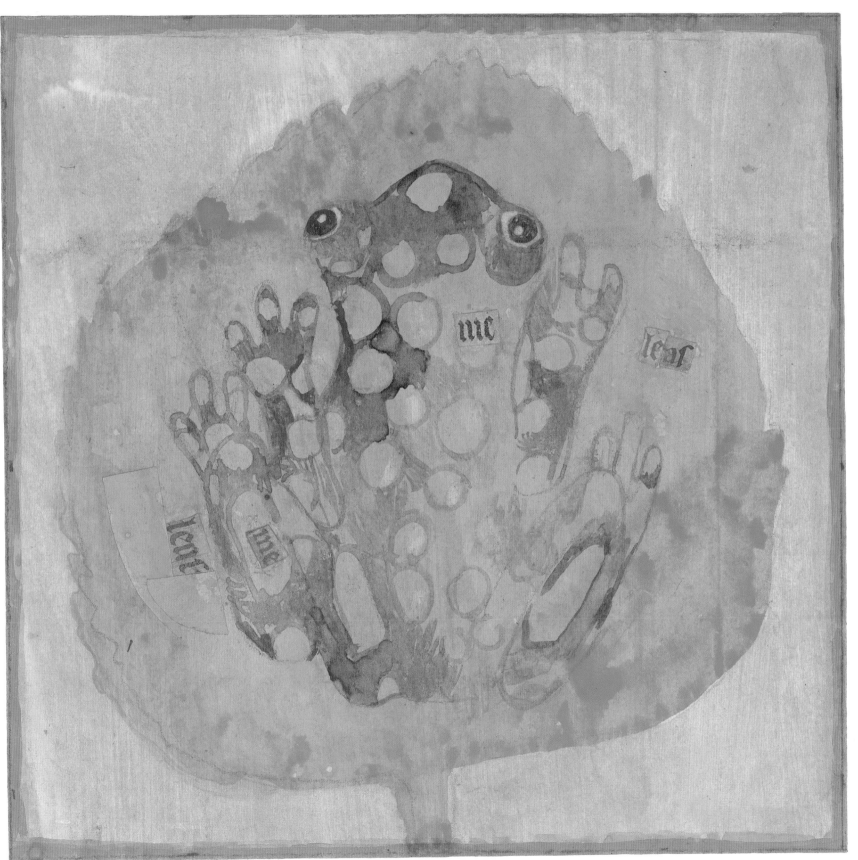

The Newt

Orange nose.
Orange toes.
Orange chin.
Orange skin.
Orange tail.
Orange newt.
Orange you cute
In your bright orange suit.

The Wood Frog

I am a frozen frogsicle.
I froze beneath a logsicle.
My mind is in a fogsicle
Inside this icy bogsicle.

My temperature is ten degrees.
I froze my nose, my toes, my knees.
But I don't care, I feel at ease,
For I am full of antifreeze.

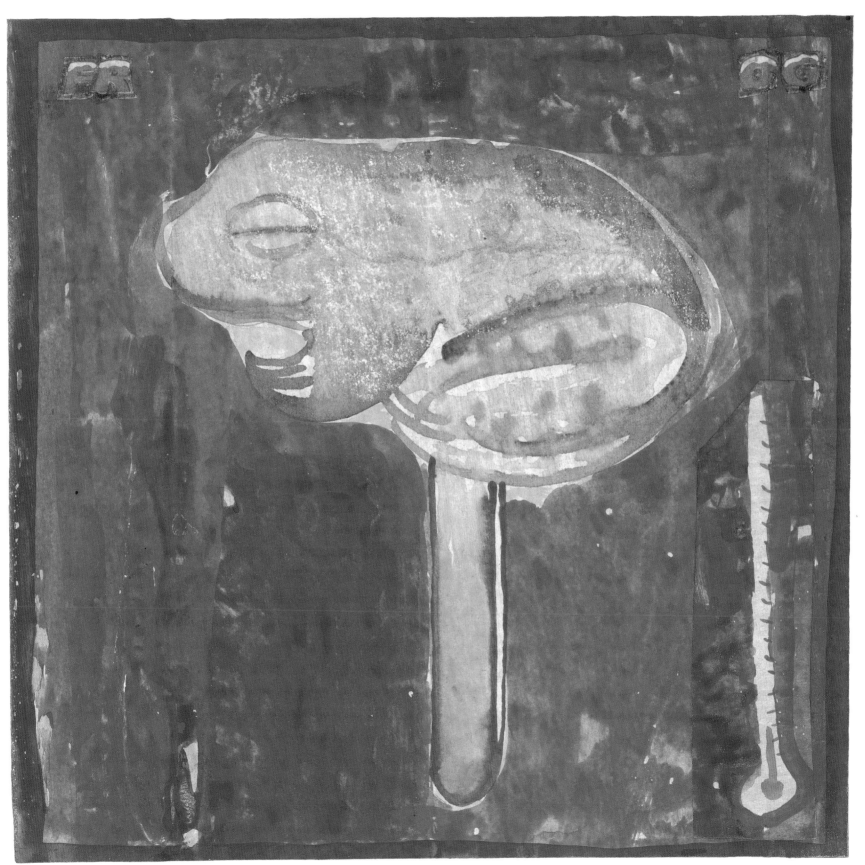

39

The Red-Eyed Tree Frog

Tomato eyes.
Catches flies.

Orange toes.
Loves to pose.

Matchstick legs.
Hatches from eggs.

Swallows bugs.
Lives on T-shirts and coffee mugs.

The Bullfrog

Polli-wogger,
Bobby-bogger.
Billy-bellow,
Mellow-fellow.
Hedda-hopper,
Freddy-flopper.
Jimmy-swimmy,
Timmy-shimmy.
Sammy-summer,
Jug-o'-rummer,
Jug-o'-rummer.

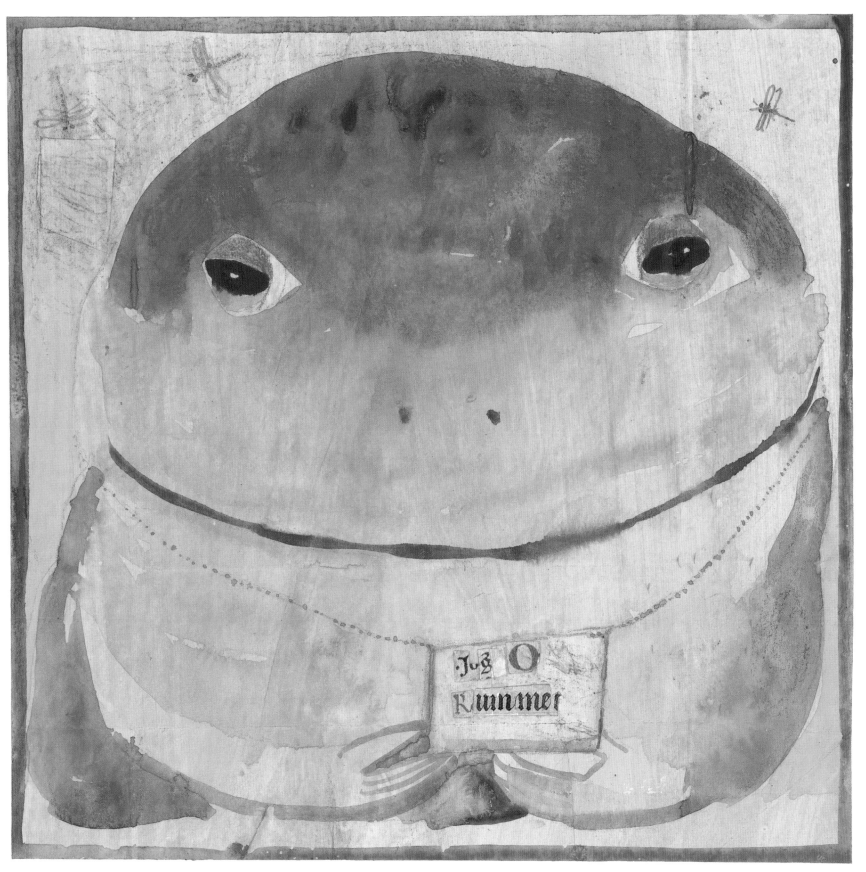

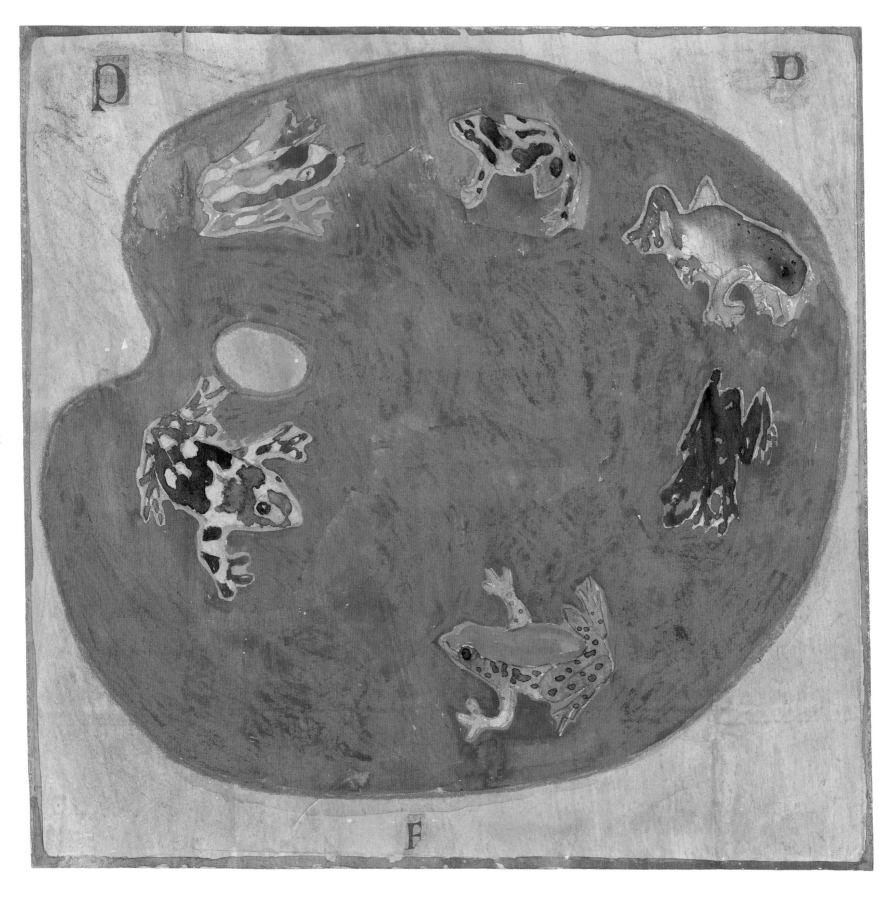

The Poison-Dart Frogs

Brown with oval orange spots.
Crimson mottled black with blots.
Neon green with blue-black bands.
Tangerine with lemon strands.
Banana yellow.
Ultramarine.
Almost any color seen.
And though their poison can tip a dart,
These frogs are Masters of Fine Art.

The Spring Peepers

Peep,
        Peep—
We steal your sleep.
In scores
        Of choruses
                We cheep.
Beneath our chin's
A thin balloon
To help our song
From March till June.
Each spring
        We sing
                To bring
A mate,
And make you stay
Awake too late.

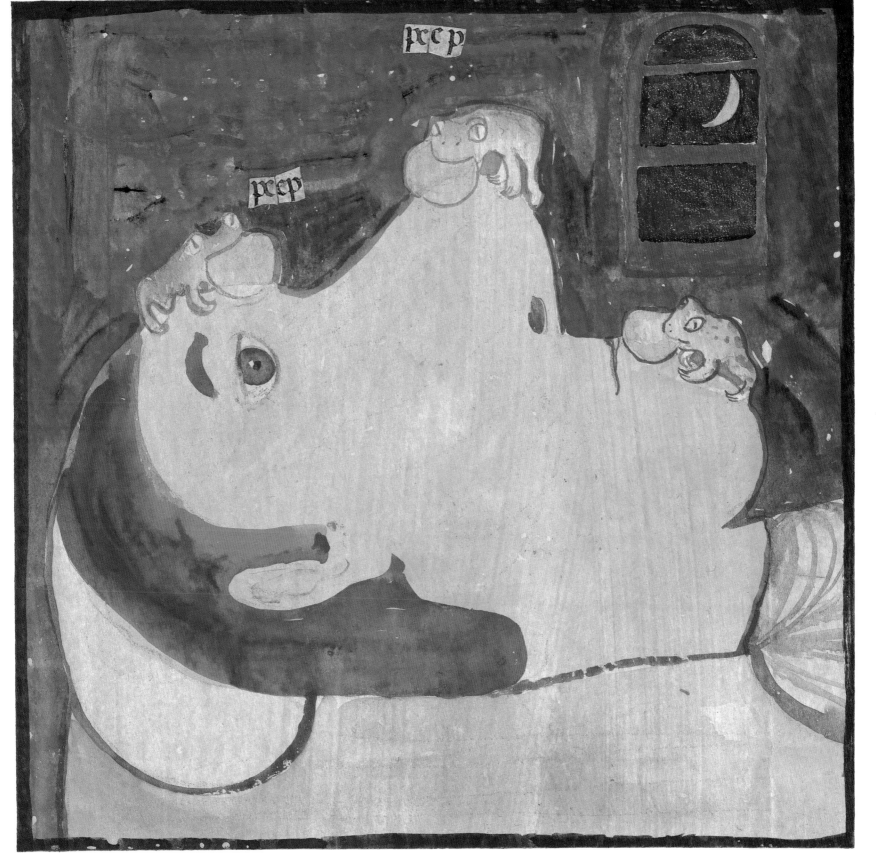

47

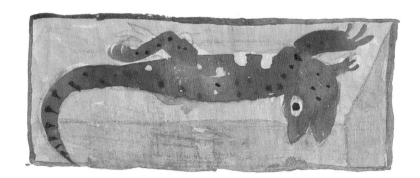

The illustrations in this book were done in watercolor on
primed brown paper bags with collage.
The display type was set in Mambo Bold.
The text type was set in Sabon.
Printed by South China Printing Company, Ltd., Hong Kong
This book was printed on totally chlorine-free Nymolla Matte Art paper.
Production supervision by Sandra Grebenar and Pascha Gerlinger
Designed by Kaelin Chappell